Poemography

Poemography

A Collection Of Poetry
Written By:

Dallas M. Quinley

iUniverse, Inc.
New York   Bloomington

Poemography

iUniverse books may be ordered through booksellers or by contacting:

iUniverse
1663 Liberty Drive
Bloomington, IN 47403
www.iuniverse.com
1-800-Authors (1-800-288-4677)

Because of the dynamic nature of the Internet, any Web addresses or links contained in this book may have changed since publication and may no longer be valid. The views expressed in this work are solely those of the author and do not necessarily reflect the views of the publisher, and the publisher hereby disclaims any responsibility for them.

ISBN: 978-1-4401-3595-8 (pbk)
ISBN: 978-1-4401-3596-5 (ebk)

Printed in the United States of America

iUniverse rev. date: 5/6/2009

Introduction

The poetry in this collection has been inspired by the
People and events in the life of Dallas M. Quinley

These poems are presented to you in their final stage of completion.
These are the original works of the author.

These poems are subject to interpretation of the reader and
Are to be viewed from a personal perspective.

These poems reflect the feelings of the author and
Are not meant to promote any negativity or offend anyone.

Some language may be unsuitable or too provocative for children.
Parents should be aware of such content.

This book is dedicated to my children.

Table of Contents

A Poet's Dream

Poets are dreamers who are too far and too few,
chasing a dream that may never come true.

They put all their heart into the words that they write,
and try not to listen to what the critics recite.

Their feelings are carried to the tip of a pen
where some dreams come true and other dreams end.

Poets can't change the dreams that they see.
They must write what's inside them, and then let it be.

If poets don't dream, they have no reason to sleep;
they have no use for the thoughts or the words that they keep.

Just let them write, and let their dreams flow.
Don't judge a poet on what little you know.

Poets are dreamers who are just one word away
from living a dream that they are chasing today.

Following My Shadow

I follow my shadow on roads high and low.
Wherever it leads me, that's where I must go.

You follow your heart. It keeps you from me.
Wherever it leads you, that's where you must be.

We follow our dreams. They make us go on.
Wherever we are, that's where we belong.

We follow our feelings which lead us astray.
Wherever they take us, it'll be the wrong way.

I follow a path that others don't see.
We walk on alone, my shadow and me.

I follow the day into the night.
My shadow and me, we walk away from the light.

Thoughts Of You

I lay upon my lonely bed
as thoughts of you go through my head.
The storm outside keeps me awake
as thunder clouds begin to break.

I think about my days with you
and all the things we use to do.
I never loved that way before,
and no one ever loved me more.

Here I lie with idle time,
thoughts of you upon my mind.
Lightning flashes across the sky
when I start to let me cry.

There are days yet to be;
days without you loving me.
I'm not sure what those days hold.
I dread those days as they unfold.

It may only storm until the dawn,
but thoughts of you will carry on.
Storms will come and go again,
but thoughts of you will never end.

Walk With Me

Walk with me in the midnight breeze,
underneath the autumn trees.
Take my hand and take my heart.
Walk beside me and never depart.

Walk with me until the dawn,
Until the stars we see are gone.
Inspire me with words to write.
Inspire me with true love's light.

Walk with me by crystal streams
like you do in all my dreams.
Be with me and I'll be with you.
Walk with me where dreams come true.

Poetry By Storm

I sit all alone in my den
as poetry drips from my pen.
The sky is all grey
and there's rain on the way,
and this poem is my only friend.

I sit all alone and write
as I struggle to see by the light.
The thunder is loud behind each creeping cloud,
but I must go on with my plight.

I sit all alone and rhyme
as the words slowly come to my mind.
The lightning is rude;
it finds ways to intrude
on what's left of my ticking time.

I sit all alone in my sorrow
as thoughts turn to tomorrow.
The day has been bad;
it has made me feel sad,
and I wish I had more words to borrow.

Love Is Forever

Your beautiful eyes see in me
all that I am and all I can be.

The words that you tell me are honest and true.
You believe in me and in all that I do.

You give me the strength to get through each day.
You listen to me; every word that I say.

You open your heart when I knock at the door.
When I need you most, you open it more.

You give me a rainbow when the world gives me thunder.
You pulled me out of the ocean Just before I went under.

You stand by my side when I should be standing alone.
When I am lost, you find my way home.

You are the one who is holding my heart.
You carry it with you when we are apart.

This is why our love is forever.
Nothing can conquer what love keeps together.

Scribbled Poetry

You try to deform the words that I write
by imposing the syntax others recite.
You recommend stanza to make my words better.
You cringe at the jargon I put into each letter.

You mock all my writings as if they were scribbles.
You try to erase the ink my pen dribbles.
You shriek at the way I make my words flow.
I defile your grammar. I write what I know.

I am a poet with improvident words.
I toss them into the oceans and up to the birds.
You cannot change what I put on this page.
You cannot deny me once my words take the stage.

I write all these words which extend out from me.
You cannot deny them. My poems must be.
You try to ignore these words that I write,
but you only inspire my poetic plight.

You try to corrupt me and misguide my way,
but you cannot erase me or the things that I say.
I am a poet who will not be denied.
I write poems with passion. I scribble with pride.

Christopher's Poem

Our child of love never opened his eyes.
He was carried by angels beyond the blue skies.
Somewhere in Heaven is Christopher's soul.
Our child of love was called up to go.

Our child of love is with God up above.
He is safe up in Heaven with God's perfect love.
No matter what happens to keep us apart,
I know I am there in Christopher's heart.

Our October tears were heavy that day
as our child of love was carried away.
God gave us a promise that another would come:
Christopher's brother, another perfect son.

Dirty Razor

Cut me with your dirty razor
to the depths no man can measure.
Look at me with hateful eyes
and tell me all your dirty lies.

Bathe me with a dirty rag.
Number me with code and tag.
Laugh at me while you depart
and move onto another heart.

Leave me here all alone.
Cut me down to blood and bone.
Go make love to another man,
then lie to me the best you can.

Don't wipe the places you are wet,
Let me sleep in your bed of sweat.
Deny me love and deny me pleasure.
Give away your secret treasure.

This dirty razor is my only friend.
It will be with me until the end.
No more tears I'll ever cry
Just cut me deep so I can die.

The Blue Sky

Oh blue sky, I know how you feel
watching the world go by.
I know you cry when the rain spills.
Now where is the blue sky?

Oh blue sky, you look at me with blue eyes
in search of a love you have yet to see.
I know how you feel watching the world go by,
for no one has ever stopped to love me.

Oh blue sky, maybe when you are gone
you will be missed up so high.
Let the rain come. I know how you feel
watching the world go by.

Father

If all the skies were grey,
I would be there for you.
It's not what your words say;
it's all of the things that you do.

I don't care about what you can buy me
or the places that we can go.
Just give me a father's love
and I'll always find my way home.

If you ever need someone to turn to,
a son will always be there.
The family is only as strong
as the father who shows that he cares.

If all of the stars had to fall.
I would be there for you.
I am your son through it all.
I know that's what you would do.

With all of your days behind you,
look back on all you have done
and remember that you are a father
who will always have the love of a son.

Kentucky Sun

The sun of Kentucky is calling for you
with the voice of seduction and a bright sky of blue.

I know your desire is to follow the sun,
to see where it goes and where it is from.

My sky is here and this is where I must be.
The sun of Kentucky is not calling for me.

I know you will go and I must stay here.
You won't stay with me and I can't follow you there.

The sun of Kentucky is your true pot of gold.
It's part of a treasure you know I can't hold.

You follow your heart and you follow your dreams.
You're lost in the current of forbidden streams.

When the sun of Kentucky starts to go down,
I won't be there. I won't be around.

Remember our love when your journey is done.
Remember our love when there is no sun.

Tears Until Tomorrow

Underneath a pale-blue sky,
a cheating lover made me cry.
Mysogynistic teardrops fall.
My epitaph is on the wall.

I stumble through the dizzy day
contemplating my dismay.
I ease the pain with phantom lies
and picture-perfect alibis.

I can't deny the constant ache
that grips my heart when I'm awake.
When I'm asleep, my dreams undo.
I can't escape those shades of blue.

I drag myself to idle streams
and listen to the angels scream.
I wander aimless through the night.
I ponder thoughts without delight.

There's no place where my tears can hide.
The truth can no longer be denied.
Here I am where lovers cry,
Underneath a pale-blue sky.

Bethesda Blue

I have bathed in the waters of Bethesda.
The angels there speak often of you.
They say that our hearts will not be apart
in the waters of Bethesda blue.

I have wandered forty days in the desert
until I came to Midian's well.
I use to be in the furnace of Nebuchadnezzar;
it burnt me seven times hotter than hell.

Write your name on my wall,
and weigh me on your balances of time.
You will see we should not be divided
as our waters of love turn to wine.

Come with me to Bethesda
where we can bathe together in blue.
Bathe with me at Bethesda
where angels speak often of you.

Death Become Me

Death is eating at me,
Cutting my skin like a knife.
It is trying to overcome me,
trying to take my life.

Death's shadow is in my room.
I can feel the creeping sorrow.
Wake me up, I beg you
so I can dream again tomorrow.

Death stalks me in silence.
There must be a way to escape.
It seems that my mind is tangled in time.
Oh, what a terrible fate.

Death has entered inside me.
I can fight the cold pain no longer.
Death is near and my greatest fear
is that my fear will grow only stronger.

Death has taunted me slowly,
lurking in the dark of the day.
Now, night is upon me
and there's nothing more I can say.

The Heart Of My Mind

The heart of my mind is not easy to find.
I search in my sleep but my dreams are not kind.

I awake from my dreams with horrible screams.
The heart of my mind often falls through the seams.

I scream for a lover who is not meant to be mine.
this is the nightmare I most often find.

The beautiful lovers who were once in my bed;
they have found other lovers to be with instead.

Each night I'm alone in this place where I stumble,
listening to my heart finding new ways to crumble.

Memories in the night run too close together.
I can't separate the lace from the leather.

I am a victim of tedious time.
I'm just trying to find the heart of my mind.

Memory Lake

I am wide awake while others sleep.
The promise you made, you could not keep.
Every vow that you spoke turned into a lie.
You just let me go with no reason why.

The places we went are there in my dreams.
They are no longer real or so it would seem.
I look up at the stars that are so far away.
We are two lost lovers, just two lost strays.

I run through the memories. I turn every page.
I search through my mind in a hypnotic stage.
Tomorrow comes quietly and slumber escapes.
I can't go to sleep. How much more can I take?

I go to the lake where my memories flow.
This is the place that I most often go.
I sit and I ponder the way things must be.
You're in love with another and no longer love me.

The lake is a friend who has been there each time.
The lake takes the tears that my heart leaves behind.
Here in the night, the lake seems so dark;
Just like the memories you left in my heart.

Space And Time

All the stars that never shine
should find a way to intertwine
in the darkness of the night
and offer up to us their light.

All these stars were made to fall.
with desperation, their voices call
through the night with one faint sound.
They fall through the darkness to the ground.

All these stars which cannot shine,
they are the ones in this sky of mine.
Even though they have no light,
I see them shine on the darkest night.

I watch another fall from the sky;
another star that cannot fly.
It falls out of sight and out of mind.
between the realms of space and time.

The Debutante

Oppressed by lovers with sadistic ambitions,
the debutante cries her tears of contrition.
Her schizophrenic heart lives in denial.
The voices inside her have stolen her smile.

Chastised by a family she adopted in shame,
she grew up seduced by those with no name.
Hypocritical neighbors predict her demise.
They socially gather and tell dirty lies.

The debutantes' dreams have been kicked to the side.
She has no place to go and there's no place to hide.
Oblivious to life, she wonders along.
Her home is a brothel and she just wants to belong.

Scurrilous men pay for her time.
They ravish her body and plunder her mind.
They envenom her heart with lucid delusions.
She fondles the strangers in a state of confusion.

She's a slave to the addiction of little pink pills.
She's numb to the acts of cheap private thrills.
She's unable to love, she has nothing inside.
She's unable to be with a man such as I.

Violet Butterflies

All the violet butterflies
that blow upon the breeze
remind me of the autumn days
when I use to chase the leaves.

With their dizzy dancing whims,
they wander through the air.
It takes me back to better days
and I wish that I was there.

Through the beautiful garden,
I follow with blind delight;
lost in all of my memories
with a feeling I cannot fight.

All the violent butterflies
fly too far to follow.
I look around and find myself
chasing the autumn leaves of tomorrow.

October Tuesday

An October Tuesday finds me here in my cell;
another day in this prison, another day in this hell.
I stand in the shadows of meaningless time
listening to the voices that are here in my mind.

Whispering demons taunt me late in the day.
I rebuke them each time but they won't go away.
My sanity wanders down dark, dreary halls
while I lie in my bed and stare at my walls.

This October Tuesday has given me pain.
I can't separate my tears from the October rain.
My tears fall in vain for no others can see
that they fall from eyes of men just like me.

I live behind fences and cold iron bars.
I am here all alone looking up at the stars.
Will this October Tuesday ever turn into November?
I hope the day that's upon me, I won't even remember.

The man that I am and the man I will be,
they have met one another someplace inside me.
This October Tuesday finds me here in my shell;
another day in this prison, I am here in my cell.

The Midnight Picture

The midnight picture with a twist of fate;
a demon loose with a heart of hate.
With evil powers, a fire is made.
It burns and kills then the demon fades.

The midnight picture with a tale of fire.
Flames burn high then even higher.
Demonic laughs are heard from Hell's open door
and the screams of those who live no more.

The midnight picture with a present past.
All do cry but the demons laugh.
Demons dance and take the dead.
They pull them from the burning beds.

The midnight picture with a twist of fate;
a demon loose with a heart of hate.
There is no place to hide. I am all out of time.
The midnight picture is painted mine.

Arms Of Another

You have broken my heart to be with your lover.
You left me here standing for the arms of another.
Lonely by night and lonely by day;
the arms of another took you away.

Candles we lit once burnt through the night.
We made love to each other by the flames of their light.
Now as a memory, you come into my mind.
In the arms of another, my lover I find.

In the arms of another, there are promises made.
The words you once told me are starting to fade.
I stand here alone with my heart broke in two.
While the arms of another are there holding you.

You and your lover sweat all over your cover.
Is he better than me? Is he your best lover?
I weep on the pillow here in my bed
while I picture you both having sex in my head.

Lonely by day and lonely by night;
the arms of another hold you a little too tight.
I guess you are where you think you must be;
in the arms of another other than me.

Painted Dreams

Dreams of mountains,
mighty and high;
painted with purple
from bottom to sky.

Visions of passion
blow in the wind.
I walk in the garden
and see visions again.

Coloring rainbows
with the eye of my mind;
there is beauty around me
tainted by time.

Our love can be painted
with the colors that be.
Love is pure as the snow
in the dreams that I see.

If only the poetry
I paint everyday
could be seen in the world
without dreams in the way.

Epitaph

I wake up each day alone in my grave.
I slumber from time to time.
I am nothing but ashes and nothing but dust,
but I still have what's left of my mind.

I am still having dreams or so it seems
When I am fast asleep.
It's a little too cold for someone so old
to lay in a ditch that's so deep.

I hear the breeze that blows through the trees
and I shiver down to my bones.
I roam through my mind to see what I find,
and I wonder what's wrote on my stone.

I am here in my tomb, my eternal womb,
with an epitaph I can't see.
I'll never know what the epitaph shows
or what all it says about me.

I wake up each day alone in my grave.
There is nothing at all here to do.
I have only my dreams and my silent screams
to take my mind off of you.

Teardrops in my mind

The eye of my mind is looking at you.
I cannot erase your face.
The memories come and stir in my head.
My thoughts are all out of place.

Insanity hides in the shadows.
I feel the cold going into my bones.
Why can I not forget you?
Why don't you leave me alone?

The heart of my mind is twisted.
My thoughts are aching inside.
The eye of my mind is crying.
The teardrops are yet to be dried.

Desperate Lovers

Secret lovers from distant lands
run away with hearts in hand.
There is no place to go but towards the sun.
They give up their kingdoms just to be one.

Soldiers chase them with desperate measures
to receive a reward from all the king's treasures.
They raise up high, both clubs and spears,
Just as both the lovers had feared.

The lovers run quickly into the river.
The water is cold but there's no time to shiver.
All the King's horses and all the King's men
are closing in fast to make it all end.

The lovers stand as one to face them all.
The soldiers attack and one lover falls.
With one hundred men beating on one,
the fight is soon over and the soldiers have won.

Tattered with tears, one lover returns.
One lover is dead and the body is burned.
Desperate lovers from two separate lands
Kept apart by the Kingdoms that stand.

My Storm

Smell the rain falling for me.
This is my storm that others can't see.
The clouds are a black sorrowful shade.
This is the storm that my clouds have made.

The flash of the lightning is my only light.
It guides me by day. It guides me by night.
This is my thunder and this is my sky.
This is the storm I cannot deny.

I walk in the puddles going on my way.
The rain falls upon me with a poetic display.
The wind whispers to me a secret untold.
A rainbow is coming and there's no pot of gold.

The children are hidden behind private walls.
The rain cannot find them yet the rain falls.
Smell the rain that is falling for me.
This is my storm, so let the storm be.

Bedabbled

My wife broke her troth with a half-hearted try,
listening to the words of a half-witted lie.
I gave her my heart in a vicarious way
and she broke it apart to my great dismay.

Transcending pain is the result of divorce.
It's the hallmark of shame that breeds my remorse.
Whether I'm awake or deep in my dreams,
I cannot hold back my androgynous screams.

I dabble in laughter to hide from my sorrow.
I tried to write words my pen could not borrow.
The omens were there for me to see,
but I denied what I saw coming to be.

Someone should propose to make love a crime.
Otherwise, my heart will be doing the time.
Don't let me dabble for the rest of my years,
unable to paddle on my river of tears.

I just want to forget the troth that was broken.
I want to forget the vows that were spoken.
I just want to go on with my stuporous life
and somehow forget that I still love my wife.

Tears

There is a damage in your eyes;
tattered teardrops in disguise.

Emotion drips down from your face.
Your heart is broken and out of place.

Please, don't hurt me. Please, don't try.
Please, don't try to make me cry.

Wipe your tears so you can see
this love I have inside of me.

Truth is often hard to find,
and it's hard to see when love is blind.

Be with me and my embrace.
Don't let your love just go to waste.

The chances we have are very few,
but I'll risk it all when it comes to you.

I know the fear you feel inside,
but we can't run and we can't hide.

This is what is meant to be.
Wipe your tears so you can see.

Daughter Of The Devil

You're a Gibson girl with a gypsy style,
dressed to the nines with a nympho smile.
You have a bag of tricks and a bag of lies.
You're the daughter of the devil with angel eyes.

Your evil heart has just one desire:
to burn your lovers in the flames of your fire.
Their cries are heard from the depths of hell.
You sent them there. That's where they dwell.

You give to Satan the souls you steal.
You damn the men with a mark and seal.
You're the daughter of sin who has no shame.
Babylon is your maiden name.

The beast inside your womb must rage
to usher in a new world age.
You prostitute your global plan
and put a mark on every man.

The revelation has come to be.
One foot is on land and the other on sea.
You may rise and come to power,
but you will be judged in the final hour.

Help Me

Help me keep
my restless sleep.
Don't let it slip away.

Chase my dreams
and quiet my screams,
at least for one more day.

Let me cry
as the night goes by,
and let me be alone in my bed.

Look at me
and try to see
what thoughts run through my head.

Help me run
from the morning sun.
Take me to someplace with rain.

Leave me there
without a care,
even if I complain.

The Pleasures Of Sorrow

I have had all the happiness
that one man can borrow,
and I have traded it all
for the pleasures of sorrow.

I have been loved
and I have been all alone.
I have been in strange places
and I have even been home.

The misery of time
has been a painful illusion,
and this reality of mine
has been full of confusion.

My heart has been open
and it has been broken.
Somethings are unsaid
and somethings have been spoken.

I have traded my heart
for these pleasures I found;
these pleasures of sorrow
that have kept my heart down.

I hide all my hurt
so others won't see
what the pleasures of sorrow
have all done to me.

The Fondled Heart

The desire of my heart that I must chase
is to be in your arms and in your embrace.
You give me your love when I am asleep.
In all of my dreams, I am the one that you keep.

You fondle my heart with dirty little pleasures.
You show me the beauty of your own private treasures.
I keep my love secret. I don't tell my tales.
You fondle my heart and you fondle it well.

When my dreams are done, I wake up alone.
All I have left are the dreams I have known.
I want to be pleasured by you in ways yet untold.
I desire your love and all the treasures you hold.

I want to give you the love that you never knew.
The desire of my heart is to be fondled by you.
Throughout forever in the matrix of time,
I will fondle your heart as you fondle mine.

Beyond The Willow

The cemetery is full of laughter.
This is where I roam.
I sit down by my epitaph
Just to write a poem.

I don't know why I like it here.
I guess there is no reason.
I can't help myself, so I giggle along
With the voices of another season.

I pass the crazy day away
with my paper and my pen.
I talk to those who listen to me.
Each day, I make a friend.

I hate to leave at night;
but there's not enough light to write by the moon.
It won't be too much longer
then I'll be back again real soon.

I'll lay my head under a tombstone
and this will be my pillow.
I'll fall asleep to the laughter
of the voices beyond the willow.

Damn The World

Damn the world that I have known;
their evil hearts with gods of gold.
Damn the hatred I am shown,
and all the lies that I've been told.

Damn the world and all it's ways;
the crooked tricks that people play.
Damn the laws and prison walls.
Damn it once and damn it all.

The Poetry Of Prison

Another page of written woe;
a victim of the system denied parole.
These prison walls, they have no soul.
There is no poetic place to go.

The prison ghosts, they haunt my mind
with the silent chaos of passing time.
The poetry of prison, no man can find.
There is only the poetry of the crime.

I'm a broken man gone to waste,
twenty years in a forgotten place.
These chains on me, I must embrace
as the last tear falls from my broken face.

The prison system, it holds me down.
I can't get out. I can't be found.
The poetry of prison is all around.
These chains on me, they keep me bound.

Another day behind a prison door;
the poetry here is like each day before.
Prison walls just close a little more.
The poetry of prison, each man endures.

Take My Heart

Take my heart, my broken core.
Give it love then give it more.
Take my hand and tell me lies.
Look deep into my big brown eyes.

Turn my heart all inside out.
Try to see what I'm about.
Take my heart, my hidden treasure.
Keep it close to bring you pleasure.

Give me love just one last time.
Take my heart and I'll make yours mine.
Open up and let love be.
Take a chance on loving me.

The Window Weeper

I am the window weeper.
My teardrops fall day and night.
I look out my lonely window
with tears that are too heavy to fight.

I am one of those lonely children
who grew up to know love's pain.
I am the window weeper,
looking out my window into the rain.

This is the life of the lonely.
These are the tears of a broken heart.
I became the window weeper
on the day you chose to depart.

I am here with my sorrow,
aimlessly lost in another day.
I am the window weeper.
My tears Just fall where they may.

I am the window weeper.
Behind my window, I hide.
My tears are made out of loneliness
and I am not able to keep them inside.

What Matters Most

Teardrops laced with baby blue;
Crystal clear, they fall for you.
In a world that's painted dark,
I can't see past my tainted heart.

Take the hurt that lies within.
What matters most will never end.
All the tears my lips have tasted,
I cried them only to be wasted.

Paint my face with a broken brush.
Listen to the silent hush.
Don't let me laugh. Don't let me cry,
and what matters most will never die.

Daze Of The New

You pull the wool over your baby's eyes,
hiding the world so the newborn don't cry.
The child is born into an impossible maze,
so you lullaby the baby into a daze.

Babies can't see when they are asleep,
but when they wake up, expect them to weep.
One day they will see the truth left untold
and the truth will be worse once they are old.

If a newborn awakes in a bed that will crumble,
their cradle will fall and the baby will tumble.
You pacify the pain like good parents do,
but your child is lost in the daze of the new.

Open your windows and unlock your doors.
Let your baby be held by felons and whores.
Don't try to disguise a world you can't hide
and don't dry the tears your baby has cried.

Let their tears fall wherever they may.
Let them crawl on the floor and go their own way.
Don't let them get lost in the daze of the new,
and they'll crawl out of the maze long before you.

Odious Leo

I am he, the one you hate.
You unwrite the poems which I create.
You despise the fact that I am me.
You curse the day I came to be.

I am he, the one who cries.
You trick and treat me with your lies.
You curse the man I came to be.
Odious leo, I am he.

Jaded Writ

Flames of Hephaestus come from my pen.
They burn the poetic words of an unfortunate end.
All of my writings, I scribble onto a scroll;
those prophetic verses of my prolific dark soul.

An apocalyptic story my epigrams tell
about the wrath of the one who will send some to hell.
Apollyon, the angel, will open the pit with his key,
then nothing but smoke and darkness will be.

A virgin's stigmata will be a prominent sign,
signaling the end of the age with a sign of the time.
This is the legacy I scrawl with regret.
It's a proverbial poem you will try to forget.

This is my karma I cannot ignore.
Aphrodite is beside me with a virtuous whore.
Her eloquent smile and deceptive blank stare
reveals the secret insemination of a demonic heir.

Her child will have the power to destroy one third of mankind.
This is the beginning of the end we will find.
This is our death. We will see this day dawn,
then we will die and then we'll be gone.

Winds Of The Storm

Winds of the storm rage far and wide.
The thunder and lightning are here by my side.
The clouds overhead shelter me from the light.
It has rained through the day and it's turning to night.

The winds of the storm blow through my willow.
I should be in bed having dreams on my pillow,
but the winds call my name as they blow stronger.
I cannot run away or resist any longer.

I look into the sky and see the storm's angry display.
I seem to find comfort in all the dismay.
I stand in the storm and absorb all its pain.
I cannot stop the storm nor make the storm change.

The winds of the storm rage with great powers,
blowing all night through the beautiful flowers.
This is where I know I must be.
There is my storm. It has come just for me.

The Perfect Teardrop

The perfect teardrop falls for you
while I sit here in my sorrow.
The perfect love you gave to me,
but it was only mine to borrow.

I waste the days that pass me by
behind these same four walls.
With pen and paper, I write this poem
as the perfect teardrop falls.

The perfect teardrop falls for you
and now I cannot see.
I broke the dreams within my heart
and perfect tears have come to be.

If I had the chance,
I'd manipulate all space and time.
I'd change the way you are today,
and somehow make you mine.

Seven

I am changing my name to Seven.
That is a name with pride.
Seven will be my name
and the name I was given shall die.

I am changing my name to Seven.
That name will come to be mine.
If I live ten times eleven,
Seven will be my sign.

I am changing my name to Seven.
As Seven, I will be known.
I will no longer be other than Seven,
so scribble that name on my stone.

I am changing my name to Seven.
That name will come to be mine.
Seven will be my name.
Seven will be my sign.

The Sorrow Within

The sorrow inside me, it has no shame.
The sorrow within, it calls me by name.
There is no place where I can hide.
The sorrow is in me, somewhere inside.

The sorrow inside me, it has no end.
The sorrow within, it calls me again.
There is no place where I can go.
The sorrow will find me. Somehow, it knows.

The sorrow inside me, it's stronger at night.
The sorrow within is too strong to fight.
There is no place to escape from the pain.
I tried it before, but it's only in vain.

Somewhere inside me where others can't see;
the sorrow within, it should not be.
There is no way around it, it's here everyday.
The sorrow within, it won't go away.

The sorrow inside me has become my best friend.
I can always depend on the sorrow within.
The sorrow inside me, it should not be;
but the sorrow is there, somewhere inside me.

Midnight Lover

Violent cries deep in the night;
a woman screams with all her might;
pulling sheets from off her bed,
and biting the pillow beside her head.

The smell of sex and cheap perfume
lingers from her private room
where sounds of pleasure often flow
from down there where the fluids go.

She trembles quietly until the dawn,
still soak and wet with nothing on.
Sticking to her dirty cover,
she's thinking of her midnight lover.

August Rain

I stand outside in the August rain
Where often men have gone insane.
I have no place to be and no place to go.
I came here tonight to sell my soul.

I stand all alone while strangers go by.
They are laughing at me while I stand here and cry.
I want to escape before I go mad.
I want to forget all the lovers I've had.

I stand here tonight hoping to find
an end to these memories I have in my mind.
I don't want to be sad for another dark day.
The price may be high but I'm willing to pay.

I stand here and wonder if Satan will find me.
Maybe he's here standing somewhere behind me.
I have no more friends, so I've turned to my foe.
I hope he won't leave me standing here in my woe.

I just want to end it; all my sorrow and pain.
So, I stand here tonight in the cold August rain.
I have nothing to offer except for my soul.
I have no place to be and no place to go.

The Verse of Laughter

I wrote this as if it were,
yet it is not and shall never be.
I lived as if I was alive.
I am blind yet I can see.

I told as if to tell
yet I am unheard and cannot hear.
I thought but did not know.
It was twelve months but not a year.

I wept but did not cry,
and I cried for I knew not.
I never laughed at all
yet I laughed a lot.

Numb

A child is born to a mother in mourning.
The father is gone without reason or warning.
The child is raised in a clear contradiction
to the words that were spoken in a prophet's prediction.

The child is taught to read poetic verse,
but his mother is lonely and fears for the worse.
She goes off to find somebody to wed,
but only ends up in somebody's bed.

The days run together and soon she is numb.
She puts all her lovers before the love of her son.
The tears of the child, she is too blind to see.
One day he'll be gone and none of her lovers will be.

The benediction will fade if the child's dream dies.
His heart will be numb and he won't even cry.
Children are born into the world that we make.
They walk on a path with no directions to take.

Numb is the child who goes on a lost way,
writing the words he finds to say.
He walks down a road that ends where it starts.
The child is numb and can't feel his own heart.

The Keeper Of Immorality

I am the keeper of the queen.
I sham to light my way.
Why is there distress in you?
Don't be afraid to pay.

I am the keeper of a doited world;
the world of the insane.
I am a puppet master to the girls
who come to me with their hearts in pain.

I am seen as a gigolo to many
but to myself, I am a prince.
I admit to my blunders
but I have continued them ever since.

I am the ruler of the high binders.
This is my unholy call.
I am the martial leader
to the immoral acts of all.

Ouija Child

From the four corners of the sky and the sea,
the Ouija child is calling for me.

Until he is free, the thunder will roar.
The lightning will flash and the rain will pour.

Under his sky, there is no place to roam.
He'll take me to Hell if he gets me alone.

He can summon the power of the earth, wind, and fire.
He promises peace with the tongue of a liar.

Until he is bound, torment will be.
The Ouija child is coming for me.

Under his wrath, there is no time to cry.
There is no place to run and many will die.

Gather yourself as I go off alone
to battle the demons that guard him and his throne.

With all my might, I will fight the good fight.
I may be dead by the morning or even tonight.

My heart will be true. It will not be defiled;
and my soul will not go to the Ouija child.

Dementia

I fight the dementia here in my mind,
but I'm all inside out going backwards in time.

There in the places you use to know;
with you and your lovers, that's where my mind goes

I vomit the butterflies I feel deep inside,
watching you and your lovers as bodies collide.

I deny that I hear the moans from your bed.
The dementia has started to take control of my head.

I deny what I see in the eye of my mind,
but the book has been written on the pages of time.

I read every word your body has spoken,
then I put down the book for my heart is now broken.

Dead Red Roses

Dead red roses on the floor;
love don't live here anymore.
My heart is just an empty place;
Tears run down my lover's face.

Broken glass against the wall,
Then her tears begin to fall.
A shallow boy I have come to be.
The roses died because of me.

Dead red roses died in shame.
They felt the heat of a jealous flame.
The words we spoke still haunt these halls.
They echo here off all these walls.

I walk alone in an aimless daze,
making my way through love's dim maze.
Thoughts of her upon my mind,
lost within another time.

I tainted all the love we made,
and watched the roses start to fade.
Love don't live here anymore;
just dead red roses on the floor.

Without You

I can't change my memories
when I am remembering you.
We are two worlds apart
from the love we once knew.

I can't stop the dreams
that come late in the night.
I can't change what I did.
My wrongs are not right.

I can't turn back time.
We've wasted ten years.
I can't change what is done.
I cannot dry your tears.

I can't change the love
that I still feel inside.
I can't make it end.
God knows how I've tried.

I can't change the words
that my heart has to write.
If I could change anything at all,
I would be with you tonight.

Tedious Dreams

Uncanny dreams in the heart of the night;
I cannot escape them until the dawn's light.
I try to forget all those places to go;
those places I dream of that only I know.

I write all my dreams down in a diary of Braille.
I reflect on them often; every mystical tale.
I cannot awaken once the dreams start to flow.
I am a prisoner inside all the dreams that I know.

Tedious nights in a transient bed;
I try to abscond from these dreams that I dread.
The nightmares cascade from their emerald sky,
and into my bed where I reluctantly lie.

The shadows around me are darker than before.
They hide under my bed and behind my closet door.
Voices sing me to sleep with a dark lullaby,
then I dream of the places that I try to deny.

Away on a cloud, I am taken in chains;
Just another dreamer without any name.
Tedious nights with no resolution;
Just another dreamer in a dream of confusion.

The Sins Of My Lover

When it comes to my heart and the sins of my lover,
   things are black and white but never in color.

Half of her heart moans with passionate screams.
   The other half of her heart is not what it seems.

She cheats on me. Her bedroom eyes stray.
   Other lovers are with her while I am away.

I follow my heart to the places I know,
   but she is not there at those places I go.

The sins of my lover I have tried to deny,
but there are only so many times I can tell myself lies.

I picture her cheating in the back of my mind
   where her acts of betrayal are cruel and unkind.

When it comes to the truth, she belongs to another;
   but my heart keeps forgiving the sins of my lover.

Eyes In the Dark

Eyes in the dark are looking at me;
looking inside me where others can't see.
That's where I am, here in the dark.
That's where I belong, here with my heart.

Eyes in the dark have reason to cry.
My memories haunt me. They will not die.
Here in the dark with what's left of my mind,
that's where I am; in the darkness of time.

Eyes in the light have no concept of pain.
Those in the dark have no one to blame.
This is our fate. This is where we must be.
Eyes in the dark have no reason to see.

Eyes in the dark are there without plight.
They cannot escape and they can't see to fight.
That's where I am; under a dark sky.
This is where I belong with reasons to cry.

Tragic

Our tragic love is my deepest woe.
It's the darkest thing I'll ever know.
Once our love was laced in white.
It was the only thing that gave me light.

Now, I cry tears of blue
When I remember loving you.
Our tragic love came to an end.
I'll never love that way again.

Night Stranger

Once upon a starless night,
the wind blew cool and the rain fell light.
Where trees surrounded the open grass,
there she sat as time did pass.

She seemed to be cold. She seemed to be blue.
I decided to go to her. What else could I do?
I gave her my hand and she arose.
She let me hold her. She let me close.

I looked into her eyes. She looked in mine.
All we had was this moment in time.
She turned away and began to go.
Each step she took was taken slow.

Without a word, I caught up fast
and on that night, we did laugh.
When morning came, I awoke
on a bench which a board was broke.

Once upon a starless night,
a stranger came into the light.
Now, she's gone and I'm alone.
The night stranger is best unknown.

Homeless

Do not cry, my children;
even though we have no place to live.
We will make it somehow
as long as we have love to give.

Hope is in tomorrow.
We must hold onto that.
Remember the things we once had
and pray one day we will get them back.

Hold my hands, my children.
I will always be here,
and I will always love you.
I just can't hold back my tears.

The Blade Of Pleasure

I use the blade to punish my skin.
I bleed for the blade because of my sin.

The blade brings me pleasure and deep-soothing sorrow.
Maybe this time, I'll bleed out by tomorrow.

I use the blade to erase what I am.
I punish myself the only way that I can.

I bleed for the blade without trying to fight.
This is the pleasure that makes my wrongs right.

I use the blade. It cuts down to my soul.
I wonder this time, "How deep can I go?"

I bleed for my heart broken by lovers.
I die for the world and for my hatred of others.

I'll die all alone here with my blade,
and don't bother marking the place where I'm laid.

Jaded Time

These circus shows inside my mind
juggle memories of jaded time.

I'm lost inside this maze of laughter.
I'm inside the walls where nothing matters.

There's a dizzy dance inside my head
where thoughts of you have gone unsaid.

This is why my clowns are crying.
There is jaded time inside I'm finding.

I'm here alone to see the show.
The three-ring circus is all I know.

I juggle thoughts of reason and rhyme,
but crowds still gather inside my mind.

Jaded time has made me see
the circus came to town for me.

Orphan

Forgive me for my selfish dreams
and the hope which has rotted my soul.
I know there is chaos within me
and at times, it has a mind of its own.

My thoughts have made me an orphan.
There is no refuge where I can hide.
These lazy hands made me a poor man
and I took you along for the ride.

Our unity has been broken
and you found comfort in another man's love.
You are content with words he has spoken.
His fingers are inside your glove.

You have often been defiled.
Now, I have lost you in every possible way.
I became an orphan.
Forgive me for going astray.

The Morning Tumble

I rise up in bed
and shake the dreams from my head.
I put my feet on the floor.

I stumble around
until I fall down.
Today is like each day before.

I get up off my seat
and back on my feet.
The room is beginning to sway.

I turn for the door
and move across the floor;
but I know it's too far away.

I fall to my side
and teardrops are cried.
I wonder if I am dying.

I lay on my back
with the strength that I lack,
and realize there's no sense in trying.

Strays Of The World

We are apart and I am to blame.
I left for another and found only shame.
I strayed from the path where true lovers roam.
I went my own way and now I'm alone.

I betrayed all the love which we had made.
In the bed of a stranger, that's where I laid.
I woke up in denial and told myself lies.
I believed every word of my fake alibis.

You cannot forgive me for what I have done.
We are now strangers when once we were one.
We are strays in the world looking for a way,
walking the line that divides us each day.

We are apart, holding onto nothing but dreams.
We wake up alone and hold back our screams.
We walk empty streets that we walk here within.
We are strays in the world because of my sin.

This Sky Of Mine

The moonlight is a jaded friend
that hides from me time and again.
I look for stars that do not shine.
There is only black in this sky of mine.

The sun is just a forgotten soul.
It left me in a world of cold.
I watch the clouds all intertwine
then teardrops fall from this sky of mine.

The sky is clear on days of blue.
Those are the days I think of you.
It is the blue you left behind.
There is only blue in this sky of mine.

There is thunder in my sky;
unanswered questions do not die.
This is my storm and it has no eye.
This sky of mine often makes me cry.

This sky of mine, it has no heart.
When you left, it broke apart.
Many pieces I could not find
when you left this sky of mine.

Idle Places

Locked inside of idle places;
the same four walls, the same strange faces.
Here I am behind these walls
where men do time for broken laws.

Locked inside this place of pain.
I'm just another felon with a ball and chain.
I am bound because of a crime.
I am here with idle time.

Locked inside these walls of woe;
they can chain my body but not my soul.
Look inside my heart and see
if idle men can still be free.

Locked inside an idle chamber,
a dismal look on every stranger.
Everyone has dreams of home.
In idle places, we are all alone.

Locked inside this lonely hole;
here we are, no place to go.
Locked inside of idle places,
we hold onto the hope that time erases.

A Million Miles

A mile away from the one that I hold
is a million miles down a long, lonely road.

These are the miles I travel each day.
I travel alone as we go our own way.

A mile away from the place I should be
is a million miles between you and me.

This is the place where my heart goes to cry.
This is the place where love goes to die.

One mile deep inside of my lonely heart,
that's where my love ends. That's where my love starts.

A million dreams wake me up from my sleep.
I am only a moment from the tears that I'll weep.

These are the dreams which are only for you.
These are the dreams that never come true.

Children Of Hate

My life remains idle in this poetic pit.
I am bound here alone. With my memories, I sit.
My hopes have been tainted with the thoughts of my fate.
I've been brought here in chains by the children of hate.

My dreams are the only place where I can be free.
I know if they could, they'd take that from me.
I live off their crumbs and eat up their slop.
I wonder how long until this will stop.

They break me each day with meaningless rules.
They don't even know me yet I am their fool.
They punish me with the loss of my time,
and bring their insanity into my mind.

I hear their lies and their sarcastic laughter,
as if they were perfect and would be perfect ever after.
They are just one step away from crossing that line;
the one that's unseen which divides them from crime.

They are no better nor any different from me.
They just hold the keys to imprison those who are free.
My life is on hold until this pit opens
and spits out a few of the victims it's chosen.

This is the place where I sit in my sorrow.
I sit here tonight holding on for tomorrow.
My life is in limbo behind prison gates
where I am punished by these children of hate.

The Poem That Came To Be

This is a poem written by me.
I don't even know how it came to be.

I had nothing to do and no place to go,
so I sat on my bed writing of things that I know.

I could not write of love because the ink did not flow.
I did not write of the wind because the wind did not blow.

There was nothing inside me that had to get out.
I had nothing to whisper. I had nothing to shout.

My pen moved my hand without the aid of my mind.
I closed my eyes and wrote as if I were blind.

When my writing ended, I was able to see.
This is the poem that came to be.

You may not understand but one day you will know
there is nothing but poetry inside of my soul.

Edge Of Time

I am out here on the edge of time
where reality is hard to find.
All my thoughts escape my mind.
and all my memories are far behind.

I am out here where the sky is blue,
with my heart all broke in two.
There is nothing left for me to do
except try to forget my love for you.

I am out here with no place to go,
where rivers run and teardrops flow.
This is all that I now know.
This is where the winds don't blow.

I am out here where no man should be,
another place the blind can't see.
There's nothing left inside of me.
Prison walls won't set me free.

I am out here where the stars don't shine,
where the moon and sun both intertwine.
This is where I came to cry.
This is where my heart will die.

Antares

The brightest star up in the sky
gives me light to wander by.
With thoughts of you upon my mind,
Antares' light is all I find.

The brightest star I'll ever see;
it shines tonight. It shines for me.
This lonely star, it guides my heart.
It lights my way while we're apart.

The brightest star I'll ever follow
gives me light which I can borrow.
Antares' light is all I know.
It's part of me: my inner scorpio.

The Succubus

The succubus comes when I am alone.
I lay her down with her passionate moans.
She carries with her an Arabic scroll.
She wants me to sign over my heart and my soul.

The pleasures of passion we find late in the night.
We hide in the shadows, away from the light.
Our bodies are bound with an abominable lust,
then we part ways from dawn until dusk.

No other lovers will come to my bed,
so I pull down the sheets and pleasure the dead.
She gets violent at times, when she lets it all go.
She scratches my back and lets it all flow.

All of her screams pass through the wall.
The neighbors can hear her and often, they call.
All through the night, we rape one another;
Just me all alone with my demonic lover.

The succubus sleeps all through the day.
She sleeps in my bed while I'm away.
When she leaves, I know not where she goes;
but she will return with a pen and a scroll.

Forgotten Love

My empty heart remembers you,
but you forgot the love we knew.

In the places of your mind,
my memory you cannot find.

My empty heart is all alone.
My loneliness is all I've known.

You forgot the way we use to be.
You forgot the love you had with me.

The memories I made with you;
you forgot them like other lovers do.

I try to go where memories hide,
that broken place somewhere inside.

That's where our love has gone to be.
That's the place that remembers me.

Ravish Me

If I could only ravish you for a night
and show you the rage of my desire,
maybe I could capture your heart
as my passion sets you on fire.

You already know my secret
of how I want you in so many ways.
I long to bathe you by candlelight,
and defile you for the rest of my days.

If only I could control things
such as the limitations of time,
we'd have forever to be together
and you would always be mine.

Let me ravish your body
and give me the sex I so deeply need.
Let us make love to each other
until both of our bodies bleed.

Throw me down on your mattress
and rip all the clothes from my skin.
Ravish me seventeen times,
then ravish me six times again.

If I could only ravish you for a night
and burn you with the flames of my fire,
maybe you'd see the passion in me
and you'd ravish me with your desire.

Pain of Pleasure

She is my vomit.
I am sick every night.
Sometimes, I throw up
until the dawn's light.

She is my cancer.
I will die in great pain.
It will start in my heart,
and then spread to my brain.

She is my stroke.
I feel her inside of my head.
I cannot forget her.
I cannot get up out of bed.

She is my insanity.
I get lost in my mind.
I try to grasp reality,
but it is unkind.

She is my death.
I will die saying her name.
I lived only for the pleasure
she gave me through pain.

The Human Abyss

The system is a society of hypocrites,
and their heart is the human abyss.
They enforce laws with a double standard,
and they'll send you to die with a kiss.

Their ego erects when others suffer,
and they ejaculate with a prejudice smile.
They hide in disguise and make up their lies,
dragging your inch for a mile.

This is the bottom of America's barrel:
entrapment to all who are free;
Then they laugh in our face without remorse or disgrace
imprisoning us from sea to sea.

This is their only solution:
a number for every woman and man.
They'll track you and me with a lock and a key.
Oh, what a patriot plan!

Where is the freedom we died for?
Where is the American dream?
I'm in the abyss and living a nightmare.
I just want to wake up and scream.

Ophiucus

The thirteenth secret sign
holds the eight arm cross of time.
From the dark rift of my soul,
the truth you will come to know.

Between Scorpio and Sagittarius,
Seven images will arise.
Every thirteen thousand years
until fire falls from the skies.

At the center of the galaxy,
the lost prophecy unfolds.
Image sixty six will soon eclipse
and the end of 2012 will be told.

In image seventy two,
a secret you will find,
one male appears to bring forth tears
and end the mystery of time.

This is our secret demise,
written and hidden away.
These are the lost words unspoken,
and now they are on display.

The Beautiful You

Upon the rose pedals,
only there could such beauty sleep.
You are space and time.
You are the ocean deep.

Upon the edge of December,
you are in every corner of my heart.
As never goes on forever,
you are my beginning that has no start.

You are the one I long for,
the pillow within my bed.
You hold the key to my door.
You are the fantasy that plays out in my head.

Let me taste your sweetness.
Let me smell the perfume upon your breast.
Let us pass time with pleasure
until our bodies come to rest.

Bathe me in you passion
with kisses forbidden and free.
Be my world of wonder.
Inspire my poetry.

How many times can you kiss me?
I beg you twenty times three.
Upon the rose pedals,
only there could such beauty sleep.

Heart of the Night

It's the middle of night.
It's too hot to write,
and no dreams can be found in my bed.

There's no place to go.
Time is moving too slow,
and I can't get you out of my head.

The storm's overdue.
I am thinking of you,
and the tears on my pillow won't dry.

I wish life wasn't this way.
There's nothing to say,
and I can't stop the tears that I cry.

The darkness is sad.
Love should not hurt so bad.
I guess we just drifted apart.

There are no stars to see.
You belong here with me,
but I'll never be there in your heart.

Darkness

The darkness is coming.
Only I can see.
You are blind to the things
that are coming to be.

The darkness is bright.
It is coming tonight.
You can deny what I tell you,
but I know I am right.

You can run to the shadows.
You can hide in your bed.
The darkness is coming.
We will all soon be dead.

There is no way to stop it.
The darkness must be.
It will come to get you
the same as it comes for me.

Nothing will matter
When you cease to see light.
You will be forgotten
along with the words that I write.

The darkness is coming.
The time is coming to die.
We are just nothing.
There is no reason why.

The Man Inside

Inner man who hides from me,
show thyself that I might see.

Inner man I know from dreams,
unbreak my heart that I might sing.

Take my shell, my dead outside;
show me well that which you hide.

Inner man I know you pain.
I am he who knows your name.

Quiet Time

Quiet thoughts are in my head;
so many things I left unsaid.
These dizzy thoughts inside my mind,
I ponder them from time to time.

The pain inside has room to dwell
even when it starts to swell.
I look away then close my eyes.
I open them with tears to cry.

Quiet rain begins to fall.
I feel each drop. I feel it all.
My thoughts are here one step behind.
I remember them inside my mind.

Quiet noise inside my heart,
it's enough to break my world apart.
I hear the words I want to speak.
I hear the voices as I sleep.

This dream is real inside my mind.
I have nothing left but idle time.
Chained inside my quiet room,
my quiet thoughts now seal my doom.

Days Of Rain

Curse these days,
these days of rain.
My friend, the sun,
is gone again.

Curse these tears,
these tears of sorrow.
My friend, the sun,
won't shine tomorrow.

Don't paint me
with your shade of blue.
These days of rain
don't come for you.

Curse these days
of troubled time.
The days I borrowed
were hard to find.

Curse these days,
these days of rain.
My friend, the sun,
has caused me pain.

Voices Of Children

The voices of children keep me awake.
I can't go to sleep so I lay here and shake.

The house is full with echoes of laughter.
I don't like what I hear or the sounds that come after.

I don't know what it is or if it is real,
But I can't come to terms with the anger I feel.

I look towards the door but my eyes do not see
Those voices beyond it that are calling for me.

Only now at the end of this day
Do delusions confuse me with the words that they say.

The madness is heavy behind the white of my eyes.
I lay here in silence praying to God I will die.

The voices of children keep me aware.
I can't go to sleep when the demons are near.

You And Another

You and your lover are two worlds apart,
Yet he is there inside of your heart.

Memories of him take you back in time.
He is the ghost who is haunting your mind.

All the cute ramblings that he use to say
Helped keep you going to get through each day.

You lust after him and the taste of his drugs.
I do not compare to him and his love.

You cannot deny the sins you two did.
You try to hide them but they cannot be hid.

I don't understand why you're still here with me.
I don't need you. I can let you two be.

I'll never look back or let myself cry.
I'll stop loving you, or at least I will try.

I will not be the one playing the fool.
I can't live in a lie when the truth is so cruel.

You and your lover are two of a kind,
And he is the one for whom you rewind.

Empty Lies

You offer me your empty lies
and look at me with empty eyes.
I do not want your twisted heart.
I'd rather mine be torn apart.

Take your love and all your ways
and offer it to other strays.
Let me go to the place I know,
the place of faces full of woe.

Take the tales which you have told
and tell them again when you are old.
Make your bed of empty lies
and drown in the tears that you can't dry.

Offer me what's done and over,
but I won't be where the sun is colder.
I won't ever be there with you.
Empty lies will never do.

Déjà vu

I feel an ache in my broken heart.
It exceeds the pain my words impart.
The betrayal of a lover is a familiar truth.
This is the kind cruelty of déjà vu.

I have come to know that lovers stray.
I have come to know their kind cruel way.
My heart is just an empty well.
It echoes tales I dare not to tell.

This heart of mine is jaded blue
It colors me in deja vu.
My kind cruel pain won't go away.
It's here inside me everyday.

All The Love In My Heart

I love you so much
that my heart just feels broken.
I love you in ways
which cannot be spoken.

I dream about you each night
when we are apart.
I'll love you forever.
with all the love in my heart.

When I return home,
we'll make up for lost time.
I'll hold you each night
in these arms of mine.

Under the stars of Orion,
I'll look into your eyes.
I'll never again let you go
for the rest of my life.

Sex Chamber

Naked hearts are torn in two
in a sex chamber with lights of blue.

Dizzy dancers spin for play,
then expect their lovers to pay.

Empty thrills are sought with greed
by the ones who want and need.

They sleep by day and play by night
between the lines of wrong and right.

Hollow souls are seeking lust
before they return back to the dust.

Morning comes like a lonely stranger
when waking up in an empty chamber.

Naked hearts all fade to blue.
The sex chamber is no place for you.

Dark of Day (Light of Night)

In the light of the night
or in the dark of the day,
I find myself lonely
as my dreams drift away.

In the thoughts of my mind,
there are places I find
where angels do not dare fly.
I fight off the demons all by myself,
and look to Heaven with a tear in my eye.

In the depths of my heart,
I am falling apart.
Oh, how my heart has been broken.
I hold in my screams
and let go of my dreams.
Never again will I leave my heart open.

In the heart of my soul,
my loneliness grows.
The demons are too strong to fight.
I am here all alone in the dark of the day,
and in the light of the night.

In the places I go,
there are those I don't know.
I am only aware of my sorrow.
Memories don't care.
They are here everywhere,
and they follow me into tomorrow.

The Pain I Keep

Another man took my bride
and put himself deep inside.
In the bed where we shared dreams,
they now share orgasmic screams.

A man who came from dirty streets
defiled my bride on virgin sheets.
He ravished her in such a way,
too gross for me to write or say.

This tainted man has walked my hall.
He has banged my bed against the wall.
This is the pain which I still keep
in my heart that cannot sleep.

Writings On the Wall

This is the feeling I hate most of all.
I wrote how I feel. It's there on the wall.

Every word there, I scribbled with pain.
When it was written, I cried without shame.

I took my pen and cut open my skin.
The scar on my arm, it bleeds once again.

These are the words that I hate to write.
Nobody reads them, so I scribble with spite.

Nobody will notice these words that I wrote.
I tried to speak them but I had no voice in my throat.

I sit under stars thinking of you.
it's a little too late since we are through.

I'll just wander along hurt and alone,
cutting myself
and bleeding the stone.

Manifesto

You are the source of my decay.
The pain I feel is on display.

My tether is short but so very strong.
This is not where I belong.

You sentence me to your decree.
The jesters laugh and mock at me.

You poke me with sticks and stones.
You cut me down to blood and bones.

You manifest a tale of lies.
You leave me here alone to die.

You give me pain I can't forget.
You are the one that I regret.

A Riddle Without Reason

There is no purpose to enjoy life.
It's only my destiny to die.
It's without reason I laugh
for the future is unseen unto I.

I have written some poetic words
but these I write with regret.
I know they have no meaning.
They are words I have wrote down for you to forget.

To whom in which I write,
I do not for fortune or fame.
These words are a wrong that no man can right.
I am a poet you know not by name.

Without you, my words are wasted
like a giggle coming forth from a frown.
These bitter words need to be tasted
so the frown can turn upside down.

This is to you I write;
a poem in which true riddles lie.
It is a poem without a purpose.
It is written with no reason why.

A Christmas Poem

Snow fell upon the ground
and gave us a Christmas of white.
The children are asleep in their beds
dreaming of Santa tonight.

The morning will soon be here
and presents will be under the tree.
So, let's go find a mistletoe
and open a present from me.

Sleigh bells are outside our door.
We have double checked all of our locks.
The fireplace will keep us warm,
and for a moment, chaos has stopped.

Soon, the night will be over.
The children will wake up and play.
Christmas day will be here.
So, don't let this moment just slip away.

Prison Doors

This prison hole claims another soul.
You can never get out. It won't let go.

This prison cell is a man-made hell.
Another day goes by but you just can't tell.

The prison lights shine at night.
They keep me awake. They shine too bright.

The prison clocks all seem to stop
when you are the one behind prison locks.

This prison stage is full of rage.
There's a different story on every page.

These prison walls hold one and all.
We are led in chains down the same old halls.

These prison men are slowly broken,
all because of the crime they've chosen.

These prison poems, they go unspoken
until the day when prison doors open.

If I Were To Die

If I were to die,
few people would miss me here.
No friends have I but one,
and that friend is never near.

Even the one I sleep with,
the lover who is said to be true;
she turns her heart away from me
and dreams of other lovers she knew.

If I were to die,
My darkest hour would bring you the dawn.
The night would hide the moon from you
and the morning sun would come.

I keep the hurt inside me
and deny myself the pleasure to cry.
Tomorrow would be better off without me
if I were to die.

Spellbound

You dabble with spells
in the dead of the night,
calling on demons
to make your wrongs right.

All dressed in black,
you wear leather and lace.
You have created a potion
without smell, without taste.

Candles are lit
on each side of your bed.
A pentagram is painted
on your floor in dark red.

The demon you've called upon
will cause me to go.
You dabble in secret
thinking others won't know.

Evil is burning
and there are flames in your heart.
You chant out a spell
to keep us apart.

You laugh at the shadows,
then drink down your potion.
You fall back into your bed
without movement or motion.

The Love Ever After

Listen to the words I try to disguise.
The truth is here somewhere laced with white lies.
Let the words still inside you whisper or scream.
Try to find comfort in your sleep where you dream.

Fondle the thoughts that you ponder inside.
Let your eyes see me and all you deny.
Tell yourself tales but know what is true,
such as the love between me and you.

Touch me just once before you depart.
Know that I love you with every beat of my heart.
Wherever you go, my heart you will hold.
You take my heart with you to places untold.

Under Orion, I'll wait there for you
until you return like I hope that you do.
I hide all my tears behind my strange laughter.
I long for our love; the love ever after.

Questions

Where there are questions,
answers will be
unless it's the question
of you loving me.

Questions unanswered
often go through my mind.
The questions of you
have answers too hard to find.

Here in my heart,
questions are spoken.
They leave my heart
a little bit broken.

Questions go on
without answers inside.
When there are questions,
answers will hide.

So I'll sit and ponder
while letting my mind wonder.
I'll let the questions just be.
Maybe one day I'll find a way
to answer the questions in me.

Alone

In the beginning,
I was created to end.
This is the purpose
I cannot comprehend.

In the beginning,
you knew my heart.
Every woman before you
broke it apart.

Just as I am,
so shall I pass.
I am a twinkle in time.
I am one blade of grass.

I was given a purpose.
There's something that I must do.
I must go on alone,
but still always love you.

My Darkest Hour

I smell the rain in the Michigan sky
and watch the dark clouds go passing me by.
All that I am and all I will be,
it all means nothing until I am free.

I am here all alone in the Michigan rain.
I am a prisoner and time is my pain.
I count down the days until my parole.
I look deep inside to find hope in my soul.

I lay on a bed inside my cell.
I've been here before when the rain fell.
I smell the freedom that was taken away.
The Michigan rain is falling today.

My darkest moment has played with my mind.
This is my place to be because of my crime.
I smell the Michigan rain in my lonely sky.
I can't see even find the tears inside me cry.

Your Bed Of Sex

In your bed of sex and shame,
you held a man who had no name.
Your bed is stained from things you did.
There's evidence of things you hid.

In your bed of sweat and lies,
he ravished you between the thighs.
You tried to hide your dirty dreams,
but not your moans and not your screams.

Your bed is wet with sex and honey.
You've made a bed of lust and money.
You scream orgasms into the sky.
You bite your pillow and roll your eyes.

In your bed of sex and sin,
you let him please you once again.
You'll moan for him but not for me
in a bed of sex not made for three.

My Insanity

The music is flat and plays in my head.
I roll to the floor and force myself out of bed.

The music gets louder then voices join in.
I run to the shower and wash off my sin.

The water is sharp and sounds just like thunder.
I get lost in a day dream and stand there in wonder.

The water turns cold as I step into the day.
I close my eyes and let the visions play.

I go to my room and see what's not there.
I can't look away. I can only stare.

I put out my hands and my insanity fades.
I am holding a knife with blood on the blade.

I look at my wrist and see the blood flow.
The music stops and the voices get low.

I fall to my bed and into a dream.
I close my eyes then wake up with a scream.

Nothing has happened and I am not dead.
I am not bleeding but the sheets are all red.

Pleasant Goodbyes

We no longer have tomorrow.
This is the cause of my sorrow.
My memories must get me by.

Since you've been gone,
I just wander along
and I can't stop these tears that I cry.

I remember the day
you took my heart away,
then you broke that same heart in two.

The love that I found
somehow let me down,
but I'll never love anyone other than you.

Now I'm alone
a million miles from home
longing to look into your eyes.

This is my pain:
I have loved you in vain,
so just spare me your pleasant goodbyes.

Graffiti Walls

Underneath the rain that falls,
I sleep against graffiti walls.
There is no place for me to go.
These empty streets are all I know.

On graffiti walls, I write my name.
I am he that you can blame.
Graffiti walls are all I see.
There's no other place for me to be.

In the darkest hour of the night,
I read the wall on which I write.
Graffiti walls are all I see.
Graffiti walls are part of me.

Underneath the pain that calls,
I sit against graffiti walls.
I draw the things that haunt my sleep.
I share the things I cannot keep.

This is where I have to be.
It's the only place where I am free.
I am here beside graffiti walls
to keep myself from prison halls.

The Purple Place

The purple place has no chains to hold,
only a river of life and streets of gold.
Angels sing of God's light and grace.
All sins are forgiven in the purple place.

The purple place has no prison walls,
only beautiful castles twelve stories tall.
There is only one language and only one race.
We are all the same in the purple place.

In the purple place, there is no rain;
There is no sorrow. There is no pain.
The garments are white; made of satin and lace.
Nobody dies in the purple place.

This is the place not all will see.
This is the place not all will be.
This is the truth not all will embrace.
But this is the color of the purple place.

Dreams Of The Heart

I no longer walk into your beautiful dreams.
The memories of me, you no longer retrieve.
My love was true but you chose to depart.
You still walk around in the dreams of my heart.

Time plays tricks on the memories I hold.
You now love another and my dreams go untold.
The days go by slow as I watch myself fade.
You erased all the love which our bodies once made.

I no longer walk in the dreams of your heart.
I forgot all the reasons why we had to part.
These memories of you, I can never deny,
but you love another. That's where your love lies.

I can no longer walk into your beautiful mind.
Memories of me, you can no longer find.
My love was once true but now you are gone.
You're in love with another, so my heart must go on.

Love Me

This is my heart.
I give it to you.
It has been given to others
who have broke it in two.

These are my eyes.
They have cried many times before.
They once cried for others
but they don't cry anymore.

This is my love.
It has been denied.
Love was never true to me,
no matter how hard I tried.

This is my soul.
It is now yours to keep.
You can love me forever
or again make me weep.

This is Just me.
This is all that I know.
Love me forever
or Just let me go.

Illusion

Memories of you hide in my mind.
That's all that you are: an illusion in time.

Feelings I felt once deep in my heart,
they are nothing but shadows lost in the dark.

Let's not pretend that we are still more than friends.
It's not an illusion. Our love had to end.

I use to deny what I use to fear.
I denied myself love. I denied it was there.

I found that my heart had no place to go.
The illusion I made had taken control.

Perfect reality I could not ignore.
I was part of an illusion but I can't be no more.

Pretend all you may then look deep inside.
Look at the truth you have wanted to hide.

The memories of you all make this conclusion:
You do not love me so let's end this illusion.

Words Once Spoken

I broke her heart and then I broke mine.
My world fell apart one word at a time.

I made her cry. I made her tears tumble.
I watched them fall. I felt my heart crumble.

I tried to take back the words that I'd spoken,
but it was too late. Her heart was already broken.

There were so many promises that we had made.
I had to watch them as they started to fade.

I'm alone once again with no one to hold.
I'm alone in a world that is crimson and cold.

The demons around me use suicide to taunt me.
The voices get louder and then start to haunt me.

I run down the hall to my white padded cell.
We are two worlds apart and I am in Hell.

I broke her heart and she walked away.
I said it all. She had nothing to say.

The Burning Heart

My heart's in the fire.
The smoke's in the air.
In the flames of desire,
my heart burns with despair.

My heart's in the flames
becoming ashes and dust.
We didn't feel the same
when it came to passion and trust.

A river of tears
you made my heart cry.
This is the river
that never runs dry.

My heart feels the pain
as it burns in the flames.
I loved you in vain.
I will burn with my shame.

The flames of today
may not burn me tomorrow,
but my heart will be there
in the depths of my sorrow.

99 Days In The Valley

This is the valley where men go to die.
Around me are mountains that reach into the sky.

This is the valley where men have no name.
I'm just a stranger in this valley of pain.

This is the valley where time never ends.
The memories I have are now my best friends.

My days in the valley, I recall with regret.
This is the place I long to forget.

99 Days in the valley, that's where I have cried.
This is the valley where all hope has died.

This is the place where I have been broken.
This is the valley that my heart has chosen.

Deep in this valley, that's where I am bound.
This is the place where the lost are not found.

This is the valley, I came here alone.
I can never return to the place I call home.

Open The Vault

Your heart's in a vault
where nobody can break it,
but I am in love
and I'm here to take it.

I am a thief
and I'll soon be your lover.
I will not open the vault
to break your heart like the others.

I want to be yours.
Give me a chance.
Open your vault.
Let me into your pants.

Trust in the love I offer to you.
Let me go to the place no one has ever been to.
Let me find the treasure your vault holds.
Open the vault. Let your true love unfold.

Open the vault where your broken heart hides.
Open your vault. Let me inside.
Let me be yours and I'll take you away;
away from the prison that holds you each day.

Open the vault. Give your love to me.
Open the vault and let yourself see.
Trust in the love that makes your vault open,
and I'll give you the love that won't leave your heart broken.

Picture Perfect

You discolored the picture
of our perfect love;
the same picture we painted
that others dreamt of.

The picture is jaded
with the colors we made.
The beautiful pictures
have started to fade.

The picture we painted
was perfect through time.
We colored it beautiful
with your heart and mine.

The picture was there
for all other lovers to see.
You discolored the picture
when you left me.

So, go paint a picture
with your colorful lovers.
Frame your painting
with your sheets and your covers.

Discolor our picture,
the one meant to be.
Love painted it perfect
when you once loved me.

Nights At The Round Table

I ponder the thoughts that make me unstable,
just another lonely night here at the round table.
With you on my mind and the stars overhead,
I ponder the words that you have said.

I think of the things that true lovers do,
I think of the love between me and you.
You deny what we feel; you deny what we've known.
At the round table, I ponder alone.

I offer my heart, the one you have broken.
I promise you love with the words I have spoken.
The nights find me crying when you are not here.
At the round table, I shed every tear.

When darkness falls, the table's my bed.
When the dawn comes, I raise up my head.
I look out the window and look at the sun.
A new day begins and the darkness is done.

I ponder the night I spent without you.
My tears are on the table and my heart's broke in two.
With you on my mind, I am no longer able
to spend one more night at the round table.

Shadow Monsters

The night is a friend with a dysfunctional soul.
I lay in my bed. I lay in my woe.

The moonlight creeps in and I start to see
all of the shadows that are here to haunt me.

I curse them with whispers and stand up to fight.
I do not scare them. They step into the light.

My body gets weak as I try not to hide.
I cannot run from the ones by my side.

All through the night, the shadows abuse me.
I fall to the floor and hope they will lose me.

The morning comes and finds me without sleep.
The night starts to end while I start to weep.

The monsters will return again, so I dread.
That's why a bullet must go through my head.

Avaunt Darkness

The cold breath of loneliness is upon me.
Fate painted the color of darkness I see.
I feel the pain of love inside my soul.
The avaunt darkness has come to be.

The flames of depression burn bright.
The medication no longer eases the pain.
Love is a cruel emotion.
It is the sickness that drove me insane.

The hands of dead men pull me.
I am twisted into a private hell.
The gate is closed behind me.
I am here where the demons once fell.

My heart is cold to the touch.
I have no friend or lover to hold.
The avaunt darkness is my curse.
My pain will never fully be told.

The tears I cry will drown me.
The madness will never let my mind go.
The avaunt darkness is inside me.
Loneliness colors me cold.

Where Lions Sleep

I seem to sow the things I reap
In the bed I made where lions sleep.

The jungle walls have made me prey
As I hurry on along my way.

The jungle sun shines down on me.
I must run. I am never free.

I'm in a place that makes me weep.
I wake up here where lions sleep.

I go to bed where lions dwell.
I'm here alone with tales to tell.

I deny the things that I can see.
Where lions sleep, so shall I be.

The Mighty Pen

The mighty pen writes your name.
It writes of love. It writes in vain.

The ink inside the pen will dry.
One day the mighty pen will die.

Until that day, the pen will write
All through the day into the night.

The mighty pen will write for me.
It will write my words that come to be.

Soon the ink will cease to flow.
The mighty pen is all I know.

The mighty pen will write no more.
It will fall upon my dirty floor.

All my words will cease to be
When the pen no longer writes for me.

Memory Of You

I am a victim of passing time.
I forget the things inside my mind.
All of my thoughts seem to undo,
Except for the ones that remind me of you.

I can never let go of the love we once made.
All other memories find some way to fade.
I cannot escape the love we let go.
It always stays with me. Those memories flow.

I must find a way to just carry on
And forget the love that is now somehow gone.
I must find a way to let my heart heal,
And forget all the love that it use to feel.

I am a victim of love's cold, cruel way.
It won't let me forget. It haunts me today.
So I'll try to forget you and put you behind me,
but I'll never be able to let love rewind me.

Poem of Circumstance

Twisted bipolar demon within;
blade on my wrist and guilty of sin.

Chained to dementia and voices intrude;
telling me secrets that I could not subdue.

Pain grips my mind and colors collide;
painting myself where feelings abide.

Edge of a knife on the edge of my heart;
Stopping the blade before death can start.

Ache of my ego and a dark diamond soul;
I ravish myself beyond my control.

I gasp for the air that I cannot see;
twisting my thought until my poems must be.

I break my world open with the end of a spoon;
rocking myself under a dead ruby moon.

I hold myself hostage in a dungeon I made,
inside of my head without a key for the cage.

Just let me just be so I can go on,
twisted and tormented with what I did wrong.

The Words I Write

The greatest work I'll ever write
Is the one I write for you tonight.

Inspired by the love you show,
A poem is born within my soul.

I write for you and what you do.
I write because our love is true.

The greatest love is in my heart.
It is my light when all is dark.

I know you'll never make me cry
Until your body lays down to die.

Our love will never have an end.
We'll find a way to love again.

We'll find each other in the light,
And read these words that I now write.

Blackened Love

Blackened love my heart has heard.
It cries in pain with your every word.

Love has turned and gone away.
It's a faded dream of yesterday.

What sacrifice must one man give?
Will I have love again or cease to live?

This is silent hurt I share alone.
This is the blackest love I've ever known.

Blackened love turned my brown eyes red
with little white lies that lovers said.

Without a heart, I'm falling fast
into the pit where love don't last.

Blackened love is chained to me,
It's blinded me so I can't see.

My broken heart cries itself to sleep.
Blackened love has made me weep.

This is why you see me cry.
This is why my tears don't dry.

Twisting Blades Of Life

Cease all of you heart-aches,
you twisting blades of life.
You have cut me with your words,
deeper than any knife.

Cease all of you troubles.
I demand my mental rest.
Let me have my sanity
or take from me my breath.

Let me know true love
before my time is due.
Don't let me die alone.
This is all I am asking of you.

It's not too much to ask for,
to have a lover to call my own
and if there is nobody who can love me,
then I guess I will Just die alone.

Half Hearted

Ever since the day you departed,
I have been here but only half hearted.

All of my dreams I still have of you,
they cannot replace the love that we knew.

You broke every promise that you ever made.
The trust that I gave you was always betrayed.

When you left, you told me your lies.
You said that you loved me with half-hearted eyes.

I gave you my love in so many ways,
with my private affections and public displays.

Without any reason, we drifted two worlds apart.
You left me alone. You left me and my heart.

Our love was so right and now it is gone.
I just can't believe that out love went so wrong.

I have been here before, when our love started.
Before I met you, I was only half hearted.

Ashes And Dust

I turn to dust a little each day.
Soon the wind will blow me away.

You will not remember the words that I wrote.
You will not remember the words I once spoke.

All of my ashes will soon cease to be,
Then there will be nothing to remind you of me.

I will go to a place where I can find sleep,
And you will be here with tears that you weep.

You will forget me, so let the winds blow.
I am just dust and with dust I will go.

You And Your Money

I'm tired of money and all it's become.
I wish we could live in this world without none.

The rich are no better than those who are poor.
You'll find when we die, we have no less or no more.

Money means nothing when we come to the end.
You may even find it costs you family and friends.

I'm tired of people pretending to care
And ignoring the ones who need help here.

I wish we would burn every nickel and dime,
And let money fade into the depths of our mind.

I'm tired of money that is hoarded away.
Hypocrites hide it from the light of the day.

They throw away money on meaningless thrills,
And mock all the people who can't pay their bills.

I'm tired of money and what money can do,
But most of all, I'm tired of you.

Spring

The flowers are anxious to bloom
as winter passes away.
The sky is filled with sunshine
and the children have come out to play.

Spring is here at last
and lovers are out holding hands.
Romance is in the air.
and time has shifted the sands.

The grass is a bright paisley green.
Spring finally came.
This is the birth of a season.
This is the season of spring.

For The Sake Of My Heart

I sleep away a sunny day
With nothing else to do.
I have no reason to leave my bed
As long as I dream of you.

I know I'll never have you to hold.
This is as close as we'll ever be.
I'll let the day just pass me by,
And I'll pretend you are here with me.

I'll block out the fact that you are taken,
And belong to another man.
I won't let you leave these arms of mine.
I'll hold you as long as I can.

I'll sleep away all of my days,
Pretending that you are mine.
I'll try to deny that you have moved on,
And left my heart behind.

Broken Love

Beautiful eyes could make you blue
if you love and love so true.
Even memories can make you cry
if you remember a love like I.

All the lovers I use to know,
they left my heart out in the snow.
In my dreams, that's where I hide.
No one can see my pain inside.

If I awake and you're away,
beautiful eyes do not see me today.
Beautiful eyes have made me blue.
Our love is broken and divided by two.

Key To My Heart

You once had a key
that went to my heart,
but it no longer fits
since we've been apart.

The lock has been changed.
The door will not open.
My heart is not yours;
In fact, it's still broken.

I am no longer there
for you to hurt.
My heart deserves better.
Your key does not work.

Just let me go.
Stay out of my head.
I don't want to remember
the things we once did.

This is my heart.
It's under new lock and key.
Never again will you break
this heart inside me.

Shy

What's meant to be
is not meant for me.
Maybe, it's because I'm so shy.

I just hang around,
letting life get me down.
I don't even understand why.

I can't look in the eyes
of the girls walking by.
My face turns three shades of red.

I know they don't care
if I'm even there.
Maybe, it's something not said.

Love

Love rots you from within.
It is a cancer underneath the skin.

There is no purpose for it to be.
There has never been love for me.

Love is a twisted waste of time.
It corrupts your heart, body, and mind.

Love is what keeps me alone.
I cry the tears that go unknown.

Love makes you ache and love makes you cry.
Love is no reason for a man to die.

Love is a disease without a cure.
It's even worse when love is pure.

Love doesn't last. It only fades.
You can never keep the love you've made.

You awake one day and love is gone.
You don't know why it all went wrong.

There is no answer to this dismay.
Love was never meant to stay.

Grounded For Life

The surface of the earth
Is on that which I stand.
I am grounded for life
With a pen in my hand.

I am here for a reason,
Which I do not know.
Perhaps I balance the equation
When I let my words flow.

The life of a poet
Is a mysterious wonder.
It can be a dangerous spell
That one can fall under.

All that I offer
Is what you see on the page;
Words that are written
From where I stand on the stage.

Positive Universe

The beauty of space is ugly and cold.
It's hiding a secret that no man can be told.

The positive universe spins us around.
Sometimes we end up where we are down.

Tragedy is beautiful in the eye that beholds;
Watching the suffering as it unfolds.

The positive universe lets it all be.
Sometimes we're blind to the things that we see.

We try to find answers to explain our delusion,
But the positive universe stares with confusion.

Pain never fades in the cycle we know.
The positive universe is just a black hole.

We can't stop the stars that are falling from space.
The positive universe is a negative place.

Strangers By My Side

You doubt the talent in the words that I write.
You won't stand beside me if it comes down to a fight.

You'd rather walk away until the money flows,
But you'll never see where any of my money goes.

You laugh at me. You put me down.
I'll remember that when you come around.

One day my dream will be real. You will see,
And I'll remember what you said to me.

You don't even help me when I need it most.
You treat me like I'm a forgotten ghost.

Don't ever try to say you cared.
I'm not dumb. I was there.

We'll part ways and I'll go abide
With those who were standing there by my side.

Keep your words and just let me be.
I never knew you and you never knew me.

Our President

He's the worst president that we ever elected,
Dictating the world with his image erected.

He made the constitution void with the stroke of his pen.
We can't buy, sell, or trade without a mark on our hand.

He makes money off the oil that we can't afford,
And then walks amongst us like he is our lord.

He watches our jobs as they are taken away.
He don't even care. He has nothing to say.

He pretends there is peace while he declares holy war.
He's worst than Sadaam or Hitler before.

Now we're all terrorists until proven untrue.
He took away rights from me and from you.

He's left more children behind than anyone can see.
He puts christians in prison and no one is free.

I can't understand how such a man comes to power.
He will control us if we just let him devour.

I'll be glad when he's judged and lays down to die.
I'll be glad when it's over and he has no place to hide.

He is the reason mothers are crying.
He is the reason America's dying.

End Of The Rainbow

I'm at the end of the rainbow.
I'm at the end of my road.
My journey is over,
And there was no pot of gold.

The colors have faded
That were once in the sky.
I wasted my time
On what was only a lie.

I'm at the end of my dream.
I'm at the end of the day.
I have no place to go.
I have nothing to say.

The One I Can't Have

Her voice echoes inside me.
Her eyes melt me down to the bone.
She must not know how I feel.
It's better that I suffer alone.

I can't help but notice her smile,
And the way her hair falls on her face.
The way she walks and the way she talks
Can make a man's lonely heart race.

Her beauty is overwhelming
But I am too shy to say.
She always seems to cross my path
As I stumble through the day.

If she is only a dream,
I never want to be awakened.
I only wish that she were mine,
And wasn't already taken.

Into My Mind

Enter my mind and see what I see.
I see the things that I know should not be.

Enter my matrix and examine my head.
Take me to places where the madness is dead.

Help me find comfort and help me to hide.
Don't let me remember these thoughts deep inside.

Erase what I know and open my mind.
Enter my mind and tell me what you find.

Whisper to me the thoughts that are true.
I will only believe the words that come forth out of you.

So don't tell me stories. Don't utter white lies.
Enter my mind and silence my cries.

Don't Blame me

Don't blame me for the words you are reading
Or I'll cut my wrist and you can watch as I'm bleeding.

Don't tell me I'm right when I know I am wrong.
Don't take me off of the drugs I am on.

Don't take me to places I don't want to find.
Don't listen to the thoughts I think in my mind.

I'll go to my room and lay down on my bed.
I won't blame you for what the voices have said.

Don't blame me for the games that you play.
You don't even know what I'm trying to say.

I write down these words that I have in my mind,
But my pen and my paper have just wasted your time.

Unwritten

These are the words that cannot be written.
They cannot be taken.
They can only be given.

They cannot be put down on paper to see.
They cannot be erased.
They can never come to be.

These are the words that are not to be spoken.
They cannot be bent.
They cannot be broken.

These are the words even angels don't say.
They cannot be written.
They must be what they may.

Work

This is my work. This is who I must be.
Eight hours in a factory will never be me.

This is my labor. I work every letter.
Let's see you do it if you think you can do better.

Life is my time clock and then I am done.
I may write seven books or I may write only one.

I'll never be paid as much as I should.
I don't care what you say. I know I am good.

You keep all the money and keep all the fame.
I'm still a poet even if you don't know my name.

All that I am and all I will be,
Will come from my pen and that within me.

Then I will die and I will have no regret.
You will either remember or chose to forget.

My words will live on and they shall not die.
This is my work and it will get me by.

December's Comet

A comet is falling.
The four horsemen are calling.
How many will be left alive?

The month of December
Will be a month to remember.
Will anyone even survive?

There is no place to run.
The apocalypse has begun.
When will Babylon rise?

The end is near
But the world will be here.
Why is that a surprise?

The comet is flying.
Soon we'll be dying.
Maybe we should take time to pray.

There will be no place to turn
When the earth starts to burn.
Will you be ready for such a day?

There Is Lonely

There is lonely.
Another lover is lost.
The price is too high.
I cannot cover the cost.

There are tears on my face.
There are tears on the floor.
I cannot go on
Without love anymore.

The memories hurt
When they go through my mind;
Remembering lovers
From a better place and time.

My heart cannot heal.
It will forever be broken.
I can't even recall
What all has been spoken.

There is lonely.
Another lover is gone.
This time it's over.
I cannot go on.

A Day In The Life

A day in the life
And it's a day full of sorrow.
I'm all out of time
And there's no more time to borrow.

I fought the good fight
And now it's my turn to go.
The ending is clear to me
And it's my deepest woe.

The book has been written.
My check has come due.
It's time to pay the piper
And all of my days are now through.

As I close my eyes,
Life flashes in my head.
I say my last word
And wait to die in my bed.

A day in the life
And it's the last day I'll know.
I'm all out of time
And it's my turn to go.

Purgatory

Something is wrong with my mind.
My thoughts all fade to black.
My memories won't rewind,
And I fear they will never come back.

Something is wrong with my heart.
The blood won't let it beat.
It's too hard to circulate,
So I have to elevate my feet.

Something is wrong with my soul.
It's condemned by God's fury.
I will either end up in Heaven or Hell.
It's up to the judge and the jury.

Something is wrong with my body.
It's harder to move every day.
I know it will only get worse
As time is taken away.

Something is wrong with this poem.
The words are not written right.
Maybe it's meant to be idle
Before it goes to the light.

Words Of A Mad Poet In Summer

I'm in love with my depression.
It's always been my lover.
As long as we're together,
There will never be another.

It hates me in that special way.
I love that inner pain.
I hope it leads me to dementia.
I hope I go insane.

Lock me up behind padded walls,
And abuse me with tainted pills.
I won't ignore the voices inside me.
I will always do their will.

Only I will find pity on me.
I need nothing from you.
Let me have my sorrow.
That is the love that is true.

I'm in love with my torment.
It feels so good to cry.
Nothing will feel better to me,
Except for the day when I die.

Tomorrow

We can't change the world,
No matter how hard we try.
There will always be war,
And children will die.

We can't stop the crime.
We can't stop the pain.
There will always be fire.
There will always be rain.

We will never end hunger.
We will never be free.
You can't change who you are.
You can't even change me.

We can't change what is done.
We won't stop what we do.
We can't take what is old,
And somehow make it new.

We can't change the world.
We can't end the sorrow,
And if we never try,
We can't change tomorrow.

Shallow Grave

Cadaver dogs are searching for me,
but I'm in a place where they cannot see.

In my shallow grave, I lie all alone.
There is no blood in my body nor skin on my bones.

I taste the dirt that covers my face.
The worms crawl inside me as I go to waste.

I know that I stink. I smell my decay.
It only gets worse with each passing day.

I pray for a pen so that I may write,
but I cannot see. There is no light.

Poemography

I scribbled my poems and now I am done.
These are my words. This is what they have become.

There is no more to add and nothing more I can say.
My poems are here. I put them all on display.

Poems are children that never grow old.
You show them the way and they do what they're told.

I expose to you my heart which many have broken.
I wrote you the words that could not be spoken.

This is the poemography on which my words stand.
I have no more paper. There is no pen in my hand.

Index